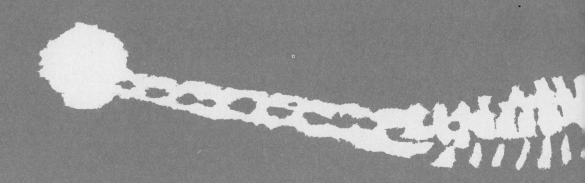

DINOSAUR ENCORE

For Hamish and Tom

The author and the publisher thank Dr. Alex Ritchie,
Paleontologist at the Australian Museum, Sydney, Australia, for
his valuable advice and assistance with this book.

Dɪɴᴏsᴀᴜʀ Eɴᴄᴏʀᴇ
Copyright © 1992 by Patricia Mullins

First published by Margaret Hamilton Books Pty Ltd, Australia
Printed in Hong Kong. All rights reserved.
1 2 3 4 5 6 7 8 9 10
First American Edition, 1993

Library of Congress Cataloging-in-Publication Data
Mullins, Patricia.
Dinosaur encore / Patricia Mullins.
p.   cm.
"Willa Perlman books."
Summary: Fold-out flaps reveal comparisons between various
dinosaurs and familiar animals living today. Includes glossary.
ISBN 0-06-021069-9. — ISBN 0-06-021073-7 (lib. bdg.)
1. Dinosaurs—Juvenile literature. 2. Toy and movable books—
Specimens. [1. Dinosaurs. 2. Animals. 3. Toy and movable
books.] I. Title.
QE862.D5M85   1993   92-19848
567.9′1—dc20   CIP
AC

Typeset in 20pt Bookman by Silver Hammer Graphics.
Produced in Hong Kong by Mandarin Offset.

DINOSAUR ENCORE
Patricia Mullins

Willa Perlman Books
An Imprint of HarperCollinsPublishers

If dinosaurs came back
to live with us today…

Which one would be longer than
this proud parade?

Which dinosaur would be angrier than a butting billy goat?

Pachycephalosaurus

Diplodocus

Which one would be
crueler than a crocodile?

Tyrannosaurus Rex

Which one would run faster than
an ostrich?

Struthiomimus

Which dinosaurs would thunder

louder than a wild stampede?

A troop of Triceratops

Which one would eat more than
four hungry horses?

Stegosaurus

Which one would stand taller
than a teetering tower?

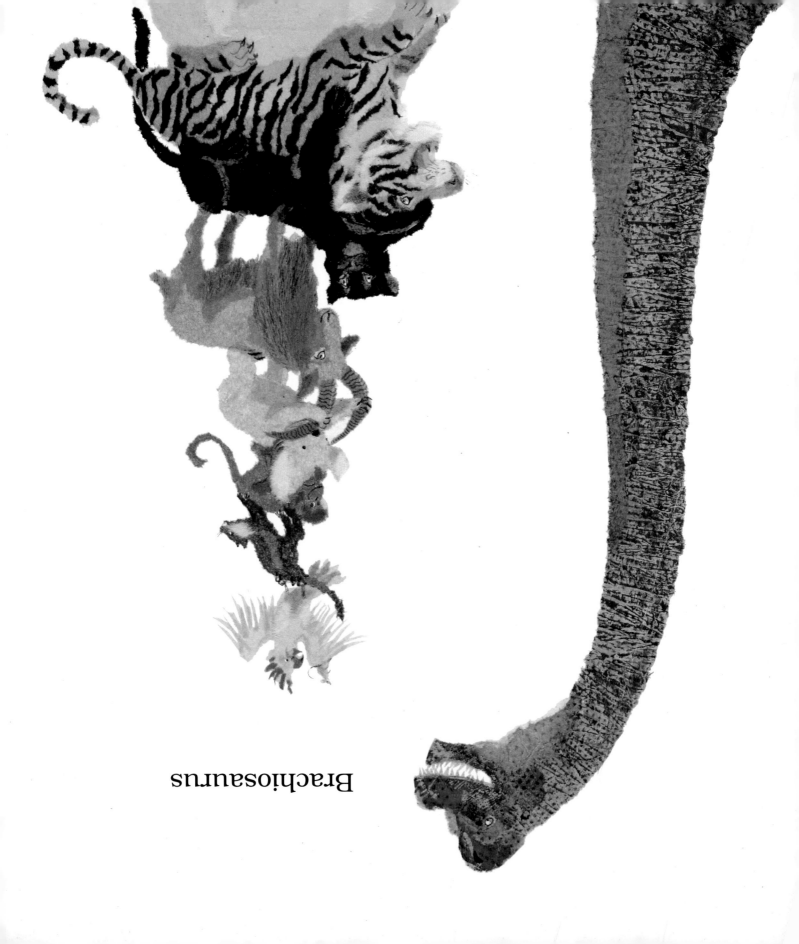

Brachiosaurus

Which one would be smaller than
our Dalmatian dog?

Compsognathus

But which dinosaur would be
two thousand times bigger than us?

Seismosaurus!

Cast in Order of Appearance
by Alex Ritchie

Pachycephalosaurus [pak-ee-sef-ah-lah-SAWR-us ("thick-headed lizard")] lived 75–65 million years ago in western North America; other pachycephalosaurs lived in Asia (Mongolia), which was linked to North America by a land bridge. It gets its name from the very thick bony skull roof that probably protected the small brain during butting contests. Some pachycephalosaurs reached 26 feet long, but most were much smaller.

Diplodocus [dih-PLOD-ah-kus ("double beam")] was a sauropod ("lizard foot") dinosaur, a harmless plant-eater that grew to 89 feet long and weighed 9–10 tons. It lived in the Rocky Mountain states 150–140 million years ago and gets its name from anvil- or skidlike projections on the underside of the tail bones. Until the recent discovery of its cousin, *Seismosaurus*, *Diplodocus* probably held the dinosaur record for length.

Tyrannosaurus rex [ty-ran-ah-SAWR-us reks ("king of the tyrant lizards")] was the largest and fiercest land-living meat-eater of all time. Tyrannosaurs lived in North America and in Asia 75–65 million years ago when these continents were joined. Adults grew to 49 feet long and 20 feet high and weighed up to 6 tons.

Struthiomimus [strooth-ee-oh-MY-mus ("ostrich mimic")] lived in western Canada (Alberta) about 75 million years ago. It was about the size and shape of a modern ostrich except for its arms (with 3 clawed fingers) and a long balancing tail. It was a fast runner and may have reached 30 mph. Bird-mimic dinosaurs had a horny beak instead of teeth and probably ate small animals and insects.

Triceratops [try-SAYR-ah-tops ("three-horned face")] was a four-legged plant-eater that lived in western North America 75–65 million years ago. It was the last and largest horned dinosaur with a large bony frill over the neck and sharp bony horns over the eyes and snout. *Triceratops* reached 30 feet in length, weighed 5.5 tons, and lived in herds that made the ground shake when they stampeded or charged.

Stegosaurus [steg-ah-SAWR-us ("roofed lizard")] lived 150–140 million years ago in the western United States. Stegosaurs were ornithischian ("bird-hipped") dinosaurs with two rows of bony plates running down the middle of their backs and sharp bony spikes on their tails. They were harmless plant-eaters and probably lived in herds. *Stegosaurus* grew up to 30 feet long and weighed up to 2 tons.

Brachiosaurus [brak-ee-oh-SAWR-us ("arm lizard")], one of the most massive of all dinosaurs, lived 150–130 million years ago in North America (Colorado) and East Africa (Tanzania). Its front legs were longer than its hind legs (hence its name). It was 76 feet long and stood 39 feet high. A complete *Brachiosaurus* skeleton from Africa can be seen in Berlin, Germany.

Compsognathus [komp-SOG-nath-us ("elegant jaw")], a chicken-sized dinosaur about 2 feet long, lived in southern Germany 145 million years ago. Each hand had two clawed fingers. Scientists know it could run fast and catch lizards because lizard bones were found inside its skeleton. The skeleton of *Compsognathus* resembles that of *Archaeopteryx* ("ancient wing"), the oldest known bird, which lived at the same time and place.

Seismosaurus [syz-mah-SAWR-us ("earthshaker lizard")]. Since 1985 scientists in New Mexico have been slowly excavating a 135-million-year-old skeleton of the largest dinosaur ever found. In 1992 they estimated that the excavations, to remove the top of a small hill, would take several years more to complete. *Seismosaurus*, a larger relative of *Diplodocus*, may have been as long as 130–160 feet.

Also appearing:
Back cover (left to right): *Ouranosaurus, Oviraptor.*
Front cover (left to right): *Ceratosaurus, Deinonychus, Tail of Tenontosaurus*
Endpapers (front): *Tenontosaurus, Deinonychus, Tail of Pinocosaurus* (back): *Pinacosaurus, Tail of Ouranosaurus*
Title page: *Protoceratops*
Opening page (left to right): *Corythosaurus, Parasaurolophus, Muttaburrasaurus*